Eat Like a Local- Sarasota: Sarasota Florida Food Guide

I have lived in the Sarasota area since 1998 and learned about many great places that I want to try. –Conoal

Eat Like a Local: Connecticut: Connecticut Food Guide

This a great guide to try different places in Connecticut to eat. Can't wait to try them all! The author is awesome to explore and try all these different foods/drinks. There are places I didn't know they existed until I got this book and I am a CT resident myself! –Caroline J. H.

Eat Like a Local: Las Vegas: Las Vegas Nevada Food Guide

Perfect food guide for any tourist traveling to Vegas or any local looking to go outside their comfort zone! –TheBondes

Eat Like a Local-Jacksonville: Jacksonville Florida Food Guide

Loved the recommendations. Great book from someone who knows their way around Jacksonville. –Anonymous

Eat Like a Local- Costa Brava: Costa Brava Spain Food Guide

The book was very well written. Visited a few of the restaurants in the book, they were great! Sylvia V.

Eat Like a Local-Sacramento: Sacramento California Food Guide

As a native of Sacramento, Emerald's book touches on some of our areas premier spots for food and fun. She skims the surface of what Sacramento has to offer recommending locations in historical, popular areas where even more jewels can be found. –Katherine G.

EAT LIKE A LOCAL- MIAMI

Miami Florida Food Guide

Alura Di Lanna

Cover designed by: Lisa Rusczyk Ed. D.

CZYK Publishing Since 2011.
CZYKPublishing.com
Eat Like a Local

Mill Hall, PA
All rights reserved.
ISBN: 9798353643944

BOOK DESCRIPTION

Are you excited about planning your next trip? Do you want an edible experience? Would you like some culinary guidance from a local? If you answered yes to any of these questions, then this Eat Like a Local book is for you. Eat Like a Local - Miami by Alura DiLanna offers the inside scoop on food in the Magic City. Culinary tourism is an important aspect of any travel experience. Food has the ability to tell you a story of a destination, its landscapes, and culture on a single plate. Most food guides tell you how to eat like a tourist. Although there is nothing wrong with that, as part of the Eat Like a Local series, this book will give you a food guide from someone who has lived at your next culinary destination.

In these pages, you will discover advice on having a unique edible experience. This book will not tell you exact addresses or hours but instead will give you excitement and knowledge of food and drinks from a local that you may not find in other travel food guides.

Eat like a local. Slow down, stay in one place, and get to know the food, people, and culture. By the time you finish this book, you will be eager and prepared to travel to your next culinary destination.

OUR STORY

Traveling has always been a passion of the creator of the Eat Like a Local book series. During Lisa's travels in Malta, instead of tasting what the city offered, she ate at a large fast-food chain. However, she realized that her traveling experience would have been more fulfilling if she had experienced the best of local cuisines. Most would agree that food is one of the most important aspects of a culture. Through her travels, Lisa learned how much locals had to share with tourists, especially about food. Lisa created the Eat Like a Local book series to help connect people with locals which she discovered is a topic that locals are very passionate about sharing. So please join me and: Eat, drink, and explore like a local.

TABLE OF CONTENTS

DEDICATION

This book is dedicated to the people from all over the globe who came to Miami and work hard to serve the tourism industry. I did it for most of my young life and I know It's not easy. Without you there is no Miami Scene; you've made it what it is and you've made it my home no matter where I may roam.

ABOUT THE AUTHOR

Alura DiLana is an Italian American who has lived in Miami, Florida since 1972. Miami is and will always be home. Her parents managed the Pan American and Golden Strand Hotel in the Iconic Sunny Isles Beach and she worked that strip for most of her younger life. Yes, she lives the whole spirit of what Miami is.

HOW TO USE THIS BOOK

The goal of this book is to help culinary travelers either dream or experience different edible experiences by providing opinions from a local. The author has made suggestions based on their own knowledge. Please do your own research before traveling to the area in case the suggested locations are unavailable.

Travel Advisories: As a first step in planning any trip abroad, check the Travel Advisories for your intended destination.

https://travel.state.gov/content/travel/en/traveladvisories/traveladvisories.html

FROM THE PUBLISHER

Traveling can be one of the most important parts of a person's life. The anticipation and memories that you have are some of the best. As a publisher of the *Eat Like a Local*, Greater Than a Tourist, as well as the popular *50 Things to Know* book series, we strive to help you learn about new places, spark your imagination, and inspire you. Wherever you are and whatever you do I wish you safe, fun, and inspiring travel.

Lisa Rusczyk Ed. D.
CZYK Publishing

*"You don't need a silver fork to
eat good food."*

– Paul Prudhomme
101+ Food Quotes That Will Get You Thinking …
and Hungry! June 15, 2022

E ating in any tourist neighborhood is pretty straightforward; until you go to Miami. This is a process to understand where Miami begins and where it officially ends. Technically, the Greater Miami-Ft. Lauderdale area is an enormous area comprising Dade county which houses Miami proper. Then, the largest county in South Florida which is Broward county.

The important thing to know is that locals will give you suggestions that may be a 30-minute drive apart and call it "Miami". I'll be covering what's in Miami proper and the surrounding Miami suburbs in this book because that's where people want to go and stay the most in South Florida. I'll also provide important geographical information that will get you to think like a local while exploring food in my magic town.

The way to use these tips is easy, as this area is laid out in a straight line; North and South. Going West from the coast is not a far-flung drive. You may only go 5-10 miles maximum from your beach hotel. Use your Google tools like Maps and local search. Make sure your GPS is on and you'll be led to places in the area that native Miamians go to.

A WORD ON SAFETY

Miami is a magic city and more than just a party town and the locals know it. That is what they appreciate. The city doesn't come without its issues. People generally know what they are; however, it's not always accurate. There are places to go and not to go. Daytime is the best way to see the city and the towns in between safely. Nighttime is for the tourist areas if I am to be honest.

The one best way to ensure you have a great time without having to think about much is to find a hotel concierge. If your place doesn't have one, there are plenty who do. Expedia Local Expert have concierges stationed at some of the hotels in the area and are worth the research.

Miami
Florida, USA

Miami Florida Climate

	High	Low
January	74	63
February	75	64
March	77	67
April	80	70
May	83	74
June	86	77
July	87	78
August	88	79
September	86	78
October	83	75
November	79	70
December	76	65

GreaterThanaTourist.com

Temperatures are in Fahrenheit degrees.
Source: NOAA

1. WATCH FOR GRATUITY ADDED TO THE BILL

Each restaurant is different. Most of the local places in the neighborhoods around Miami won't include the gratuity in the bill. However, in the areas that the locals go, but also see a good tourist turnout; the restaurants will include the tip. Make sure you don't write on that little blank line for the tip amount; it will still be there. Look below the subtotal and tax for a gratuity up to 21%. Yes, I'm not kidding. You don't want to have to secure a budget for tips. You didn't take a cruise.

2. THE MIAMI LOCAL SUBURBS AND TOWNS WITH THE BEST FOOD

The local Miami suburbs include: Miami Gardens. Little Haiti, Little Havana, and Coral Gables. Now, Coral Gables is the pricier of the two. However, I love to catch lunch and a pop up fashion show or live music. Where? Anywhere. You'll hear it and see it. Look on Facebook on the local pages for the area. That's the best way to find local events. Expect to spend $20-$30 per person though. If you're looking for local fare with a big splash of spicy culture, I prefer Little Havana for the best all around Cuban cuisine and Little Haiti for the best of the Caribbean, and West Indies and it's also miles cheaper.

3. WHAT TO EXPECT FROM SOUTH BEACH?

South Beach, or as it's commonly referred to as, SOBE has much to offer for both the locals and tourists. However, I don't recommend this for folks 60 plus and during the day only for families. To me, it's just not family friendly at night. You'll be thinking too much about strategy and movement; mostly avoidance to really enjoy the night out there. If you love the beach, north beach is quieter and less crowded. More locals and no real stupid crime to worry about.

4. HOW TO EAT IN SOBE WITHOUT THE CROWDS AND EXPENSE

If you're younger and just have to see the place there are ways to do that. Be prepared to pay for the experience and the area. $30 plus unless you find one of the small Spanish places a little west of the beach side. Anywhere on the beach, if you can get a table in season, will be pricey with an almost guaranteed 21% gratuity attached. You could do some research on places a little west of the beach and then enjoy a drink special on the beach itself. Save money, and get the experience.

5. BEWARE OF THE DRINK SCAMS

Simply put, when you do go for those drink specials, do what the locals do. Avoid all of the two for ones. That's a very counterintuitive thing, but you'll end up getting talked into a "large" two for one, and paying more in the markup. At this point it's better you buy your drinks, especially the beer, one at a time to get the cheaper deal. This way, you'll actually get to drink and finish what you pay for.

6. BEST DAYS FOR DRINKING EATING LIKE A LOCAL

Locals love a Taco Tuesday. They also love chains with dinner for 2 and 4 people. Families will frequent any place that offers these. There are several ways to find them and get the best local coupon specials.

Ask your hotel concierge

Find a local coupon paper. They're typically bright pink, and the size of a book out in front of businesses on the beach on a rack. They have all the local specials. You can find them online too and for me and the other local yocals, Groupon is our friend. South Florida has one of the best Groupons around. You can even find them for services in the spas and restaurants in your hotel that they will neglect to tell you about up front.

7. CULINARY TOURS:

Yes, locals take advantage of them. They are well worth the price and have them everywhere from Hialeah to West Palm Beach which is a popular thing to do that I love. I do it monthly on and off throughout the year and get to sample food from every kind of restaurant and price point for one $25-$30 fee and it's a great way to expand your palette. If you have any food sensitivity or allergy issues, simple Google Food tours and look at the list of places they stop. Choose the one you'll get the most out of.

8. EXPLORE THE LOCAL STREET FOOD

There are open air vendors at local art and music markets. They take place every Friday through Sunday. Farmers markets as well have some great street food. I love the variety. I used to think it was all hotdogs and hamburgers. You can get everything from fast food to Indian Kebab and more.

9. LATIN AMERICAN FOOD

Most people associate Miami with Cuban food and culture. And while that's true, Miami has most of central and South America, and the Dominican Republic. From Peruvian food to even Puerto Rican influence. You can find those anywhere, both inside and outside of tourist areas. Little Havana and Little Haiti are the most obvious, but Hialeah is the best tip off. Hialeah is in its second life as some much needed refurbishment has taken place. Enjoy eating downtown with the greatest mix of Latin American culture alongside the locals.

10. HAITIAN AND DOMINICAN FOOD

If you want the best portions then Little Haiti, best experienced during the day, has some incredible take out stands. You know you're eating like a native when you have to stand and eat. Or, there's no place to sit down. I'll cover what you can expect in the service department later on.

I would make sure you aren't going to eat and then be out all day. You are apt to have leftovers. If you think you'll be out all day, maybe order one thing and split it between you. One container of Haitian or any Caribbean takeout can be easily split. The food is typically some kind of meat, like oxtail or goat or even beef and pork with yellow or brown rice and a vegetable like yucca.

11. CUBAN FOOD

Cuban food is the highlight and as a tourist you'll want to eat it in the better places.The food must be authentic if you want to eat like a native. This is when Little Havana is a day trip. Go during brunch time around 11am. Scope out the domino walk at the park at 801 SW 15th Avenue. You will find plenty of authentic Cuban food from street food vendors to little cafes. The cafes should be investigated first for the best pastry and sandwiches. Then, take in the sights of true Cuban tradition. The elders, generations of immigrants playing dominos and reminiscing.

You simply must have a "Midnight" aptly called in Spanish; medianoche. The Midnight Sandwich is a tradition and every true Miamian has eaten this, myself included at least a dozen times. A sandwich that consists of pressed, warm cuban bread, flaky and delicious awaits you. Inside lies a bed of mayo, mustard, pickle, pork and swiss cheese.

12. AVERAGE PRICES FOR LOCALS: DON'T SETTLE FOR MORE

There is an average price for certain items that locals just don't budge on. The locals are regular people. Some with families and lots of singles. They all have budgets here because, well eating is a necessity, but eating out isn't. Face it, this is one of the most expensive places to live and when rent hovers around $2000 average before bills, you'll tighten up any way you can.

If you look at the menu on the beach for most places, it will be an identical menu elsewhere and for less. There are plenty of restaurants that cover all those colorful Miami cultures and their food for much less. I already covered the great portions for the price. On the beach, and other high tourist areas, you are apt to find the more nouveau riche food as I like to call it.

You know the kind. You see it on food shows. That high priced garnish with some food mixed in and cut in geometrical shapes. Yeah, unless you're a very rich local, we don't do that. I grew up here and never felt it necessary to pay $100 a person for the same food you get in portions on the west side for $5.

13. ADDITIONS TO YOUR BUDGET IF YOU MUST EAT LIKE A TOURIST

Far be it for me to tell you how to eat while you're here. So, I will tell you how to budget to eat like a tourist if you want that experience. Over and above your other necessary expenses for entertainment you'll need an extra $60 per day each person so multiply that for each person. If you eat out every day in places like SOBE or Brickell and anywhere downtown or on the beach anywhere between Miami and Broward County beaches you'll spend at least that much in tourist areas.

14. BUDGETING TO EAT ONLY LIKE A NATIVE

If you really want to have that native-only experience you can do it. Budget for $15-$20 dollars a day for street food and minor small, culturally-based restaurants. For breakfast, try and get a hotel with free breakfast. There's plenty everywhere. Steer clear of the expensive breakfast buffets and the ones that tout Mimosas and all you can eat etc.

For what you'll pay for that, a whopping $27-$30 bucks you can get free or self-catering. A Miamian will go to breakfast at certain spots that you can too. I'll cover those later on. Right now, this is you staying on the beach. Don't get caught up in the tourist hype.

For dinner like a Native you can get away with another $10-$15 if you do not sit down dinner. Double it still, just to be safe in case you do go that route.

15. GROCERY STORE PREPARED DINNERS

Yeah. You heard me right. There are Spanish grocery stores like our biggest chain called Bravo Supermarkets. In tourist areas or high-density suburbs, the grocery store will have a take out or sit in buffet. You will have 3-5 choices and the portions are off-the-chain along with the flavor. This will cost you anywhere in the neighborhood of $5-$10 or more depending on how much you choose. You are in control and can split this meal two or more ways as well.

Publix Deli is a bit more pricey, but if you strategize it right, you'll have a good prepared Deli meal or even some Publix sushi for maybe $3-$5 more than Bravo. The portions are smaller though.

16. OTHER CULTURAL FOODS NATIVES LOVE

I've beat the drum of the Caribbean and the Spanish Isles in the first part of the book because, face it, this is what people associate us with. I have news for you, we love our Italian, Greek, Russian, Eastern and Western European populations and their food!

I grew up in Sunny Isles Beach; now called Venice of America, Florida's Riviera. This magical place was a sleepy beach town with Tiki bars and small hotels. Now, much to the chagrin of the natives it has towering half-empty highrises. The better part of it are the Russian community and other Eastern block countries like Hungary and more who have opened business there. Sunny Isles is a pricey beach town, but it has a fair amount of locals to tourists. Most of the tourists are seasonal residents. They are more likely to want neighborhood food. That's a mix of fine dining and chain.

17. SELF CATERING

I mentioned the grocery stores before and if you really want to do it like a native, you may want to consider self-catering at least for part of the time. Natives are notorious for their beach staycations. When we "go away" so to speak, we will find efficiencies or rooms with kitchens. Airbnb or Vrbo are our best choices. There is typically a Publix grocery with a Deli Grab and Go section which is pre-made salads, sandwiches and soups. Winn Dixie is also a grocery store with a big buffet including wing buckets for approximately $13 that will feed at least two.

With Bravo, you can self cater as well as Whole Foods or its competitor Fresh Market. They both have incredible bars of food spanning the entire middle aisle of the shop. You can pay by the pound and control your spending. Refrigerate the rest in your space.

18. FAST FOOD THE MIAIMI NATIVE WAY

Yes. Contrary to popular belief, we are not eating dinner every night on SOBE or the bay watching the sunset over the skyline. We are with kids, families and singles that have normal lives just like you. Fast food opinions are still priced up for tourists in these areas.

For instance, the Burger King in Sunny Isles that's been there since I was a teenager can be up to $3 more expensive with smaller portions than the ones inland. The best ones have dollar menus. A simple Google search with: " Fast Food with Dollar Menu Miami Beach" or whatever area you are in will yield a good result.

No need to type in a specific restaurant unless you are stuck to a particular type. We do have more than just those common fast food places with a dollar or economy menu.

19. BEST COUPON AND DEAL FINDERS

Depending on the neighborhood you're in you can always default to Groupon or those coupon mags in the racks I spoke about in the tourist areas. However, when you really get into the suburbs such as Miami Beach North, Middle Beach and inland you'll want to take advantage of those local deals.

There are chains, but most of them are franchises so they have separate deals that tourists would never know of. Where do you find them? You do this: Get on the internet. Search local deals for whatever chain you are looking for. Have your GPS turned on. Just like you would at home.

We have a large Yiddish and Ireali population and from New York always. We know we love our Deli's as well as Einsteins Coffee and Deli and even Starbucks and Dunkins. There are deals you can take advantage of and stand in line with the natives! This is what native Miamians do. If you do love your chains, you can join all the loyalty clubs and download the apps before you get here and enjoy free food and discounts typically up to 60%.

20. FIND LOCAL BBQ NEIGHBORHOOD STYLE

Believe it or not, we don't all live on mimosas and fancy food. We are still in the South. People tend to forget that the South doesn't stop at Atlanta. In fact, this is the Deep South. All of the cultures we have here tend to hide this aspect that is still very much alive and well.

BBQ nights are as popular here as anywhere. We like having them as well, but with the heat we aren't quite as tough as our neighbors across the Gulf in Texas. The one secret we have is we have also incorporated culture into some of our BBQ. So, if you want to dig into great BBQ and experience the Brazilian Culture you can find one of our Brazilian steakhouses. All the flavor of BBQ with Portuguese color and flare served to you at your table in a lavish way. Worth every bit of money..

Now, the best traditional BBQ in my humble opinion, is not found on the beaches or in the highly cultural areas of Miami. Some Miami suburbs like North Miami Beach have them, but I prefer Broward County for this. Why? Less full of other cultures although they still have a rich mix it's quieter than the Miami side.

These areas are still considered the country in places like Davie, Dania, and other places out in West Broward County. When you start seeing pickup trucks and the real Florida, that's where we go for our BBQ. The GPS and Google again will tell you where the places are at the time you are reading this book.

21. TINY COFFEE SHOPS LATIN STYLE

You really need to learn how to drink your coffee latin and caribbean style when you come here if you want to eat like a native. We can't have you running around telling people you ate like a native if you haven't practiced that! Just kidding, we'll let you come back, but you want to look good when you are with your own townies right?

Okay, first you must understand that in Cuban coffee bars or places you can clearly only see a bar and no real seating, it's one of those authentic places. Step up and be prepared to wait. You may see people coming up and the barista just gives them a coffee shot, they slap the money down or sometimes a regular will have a tab.

Order and wait. Then pay and leave no tip. Not necessary. If they are Americanized enough, they may have a tip jar or if you see many people tipping then you can and it will never be much. A buck or even 50 cents is typical. They will stop by that coffee place 20 times a day. Slight exaggeration, but just slight.

You stand to drink your coffee and notice people talking to each other like they grew up together and they may have. The people will speak Spanish and just as if you are in Cuba itself which is such an amazing experience. If you practice your Spanish, you'll be met with friendly smiles most of the time. Use that coffee time to merge with another culture. You may actually end up dancing with someone. No lie, it happens here spontaneously all the time!

22. SATISFY YOUR SWEET TOOTH MIAMI STYLE

For sweets you simply can't just find a Baskin Robbins and be happy with that. You have it at home and if you're already culture shocked and home sick and want to run to the chains you find at home, hear me out. Sweets, pastries, even ice cream is something special in Miami, because of the cultures you find here.

If you want to do it like a native then follow this bit of advice. For breakfast, one day go to one of the little Cuban or Caribbean bakeries and sink your teeth into a Guava or Guava and cheese pastry. Yes, the grocery stores have them too here, yet there will never be a warmer, sweeter and lovelier experience than one from a bakery.

Outside of the cultural scene which touts way more than the gateway pastry of Guava and cheese, if you love ice cream go over to Salt and Straw. This chain is from the West coast of the US,, but has made a splash right here. Like cheesecake, Oreo and Red Velvet? Go

31

on over to Fireman Derek's Bake Shop. How about some art and ice cream? Visit the Wynwood walls for the great street art like we do on the weekends and hop on over to Wynwood Parlor. Start there and talk to people, you'll discover more from the locals!

23. LET'S TALK ABOUT THE SERVICE

Miami, in mostly Dade County due to many local-only factors, you will , not may, but will experience what most people would consider bad service. Slow service is guaranteed at many places. Now, sometimes it's due to cultural differences and how the restaurant owner values speed. Simple as that. No, you aren't going to always get NYC or California service so be forewarned right now. If you do get this type of service at one of the pricier nouveau riche restaurants, get up and walk out; it's a different story altogether. Other places that are far more local and laid back, just approach it as a very brand new experience.

24. PICNICS AND PARKS

I touched on this once before and now I'll provide a suggestion. Floridians, and especially Miamians love their nature. They love it as much as eating and when you combine both it's an experience. Go self catering and bring some of your faves you've found in the cultural grocery or even at one of those wonderful take out island places and sit among the trees and wildlife that Miami has to offer.

No. You aren't apt to get eaten by a croc or a Gator while having an innocent picnic. One rule of thumb, do it like the natives do and be at the picnic grounds and read the advisories. You'll be fine.

25. PICNICS AND BEACHES

The best picnics I've had are at the beach. Most beaches allow that plus tents and more. Just no overnight camping. You have them, just not most beaches. They are designated for that so Google those. You can by the way get Uber eats and other food delivery services that will straight up deliver on the beach.

Did you know that there are groups and family owned farms that will still have bonfires and smores? Yup they're there. Be adventurous and think outside the box and you'll find out exactly how we live here.

.

26. VISIT NEIGHBORHOOD BUFFETS

Buffets are prevalent in both chains and mom and pop restaurants all across the state of Florida. We, as natives, frequent buffets on the weekends mostly and on Holidays for sure. Typically, they are popular with those of us who hate picnics, but want the variety and savings a buffet will bring.

You can find them in everything from Mongolian BBQ to Chinese, Mexican and don't forget that good old American fare. You will find them in the tourist areas as well as the neighborhoods. This is the one thing you could find a deal at in the tourist areas as well. Just do the research. You'll spend between $12 to $30 per person for all you can eat.

27. DINERS ARE KING

In Miami, A diner is one of the most popular choices for native Miamians any time of the day or night. We boast 24 hour diners spanning Dade, Broward and the Palm Beaches. Most of us will even travel out of Dade county to visit a good diner. Diners as you may know from wherever you're from typically serve American food as the Diner is an American concept. However, here you can find Spanish, Portuguese and more.

.

28. 24 HOUR AND LATE-NIGHT CHAIN RESTAURANTS

We also have the chains you may be comfortable with if you prefer it. Towards the city, Brickell area and downtown you'll find the 24 hour Denny's and the late night Chilis and places like that. Just in case you're done with all the Spanish and Island food or just decide it's not for you.

29. ORDERING CUBAN COFFEE THE MIAMI WAY

One of the things I touched on in the food tour section is the real Latin coffee bars. Here are the coffee types from strongest to lightest. Don't do the tourist thing and order a Cuban Coffee.

Cafecito: One shot of Cuban coffee with mostly steamed milk that's full of sugar and it is meant to be strong–very strong.

Colada: This is the one you share. Your Colada will come in a foam cup. They will give you several small plastic shot cups to pour out into them and share with friends. Be aware though, it is much too concentrated to drink by yourself.

Cortadito: Clarito, Oscurito or mediano; it's your choice. That's light milk, heavy milk or right in the middle, and It's served with sugar already in it. In fact, all of these do. You're going to be awake one way or another.

Con Leche: This is just like a latte, but you guessed it–stronger and served with a tiny toast for dunking, and It's a morning thing.

30. EATING BEACHSIDE OR BAYSIDE

Here, water is water. Just pretend it's liquid gold and not h2O. There's a beautiful view, whether you're the ocean or the intercoastal. You bet your bottom dollar, which is all you'll be left with, that you'll break the bank.

The way to beat this is to go to the beaches that aren't so popular like North Beach or the restaurants on the pier like Dania beach.

31. TAKE ADVANTAGE OF INLAND DEALS AND DOLLAR MENUS

We already covered inland and neighborhood deals. Contrary to popular belief we do Dollar Manus. If you have kids or got your pocket picked a pit too early in the vacation eating at the trendy tourist places, go into any safe neighborhood and find a McDonalds and other fast food chains. Unlike other places in the country, most of them have dollar menu deals. We also have quite a few McDonalds Bistros if you want better quality at a good price.

32. BEST WAY TO HAVE AMERICAN COMFORT FOOD

Again, each and every neighborhood has the chains you love and are used to. However, you can have good old American fare without the priciness of the tourist areas. The restaurants may come and go so the safest way is to mention the neighborhoods so that you can GPS any American food you want to have. Brickell Area; North Miami Beach; Midtown; Miami Downtown, although that will be crowded and a bit pricier for sure.

33. HOTELS HAVE SOME OF THE BEST FOOD IN TOWN

Hotels that your concierge will know of, have some of the best food in town. No one ever thinks of looking inside of a hotel for food if they aren't staying there.

Ahh, but here you find the gems in big hotels. I mentioned Expedia Local Expert earlier. I used to be one. You can find one and tap them for info, coupons and freebies; it;s what they're there for. There always one in the W Hotel in Ft Lauderdale and they're all over SOBE. However, there are hotel concierges everywhere so take advantage of it.

34. GAS STATIONS—WAIT—HEAR ME OUT!

We do have large gas stations all over Dade and Broward with some of the most delicious grab and go food. That includes artisan crafted subs and sandwiches and they are yummy. The deli in some of them is off the chain. You can never tell which chain of gas stations will have them, so consult the GPS. Wawa is one of them, but that one is made for that, you will find others that you wouldn't expect. It's a way to have a good breakfast or lunch on the go and save the cash for a better meal later on.

35. WINE SHOPS NOT BARS

Wine shops have some great lunch style food. You could sample some of your favorites and go home with a bottle if you like. Find out when they have tastings and events. We gate crash though all the time in the local neighborhoods when they have food it's amazing.

36. FOOD HALLS

So, what 'sa food hall? Food halls are not quite a market although restaurants can be found there. They're more like where you can find many flavors and food types under one roof. El Palacio de los Jugos is one of the recommended ones to try in Miami. This place has been around a few generations. Just look for the red and yellow awnings.

37. FOOD TRUCKS

Yes. We love our food trucks. You can make a whole day or evening or even late night activity at one of the many cultural happenings in town. They're typically announced on all the Chamber of Commerce websites for the Miami neighborhoods you want to go to. You can find them with a variety of foods at any art or music event.

38. ART FAIRS

Apart from food trucks we like to have a flea market full of vendors at our many art fairs. You can find food in many flavors from American to Latin; Caribbean to Italian and more. Another thing we like to do is have our art fairs set within feet of a parade of shops and restaurants. Take your pick, our city is your oyster.

39. FARMERS MARKETS

If food trucks and art fair food is not your thing, you may want to go shopping at one of our flea markets. There are plenty including the Hialeah flea market and the Swap Shop in Ft.Lauderdale. Those types of flea markets are there all the time. There are plenty of others on Saturdays and Sundays as pop ups in the small towns. The more affluent areas have these pop up markets and the food is absolutely fabulous.

40. BREAKFAST FOR LOCALS

Breakfast typically comes from the local chains you have at home if you're not an international visitor. IHop and Denny's are big ones. If you want to steer clear of the same old American thing then, our Diners are our default. Both counties are littered with them. We have real mom and pop diners here. Not only that, but a ton of them have just celebrated their 65th anniversary. Some have been around longer. COVID didn't touch them because their places are paid off. Some are historical landmarks. Visit them and support the locals. They'll appreciate it.

41. NEIGHBORHOODS WITH THE BEST MIX OF CHAIN AND SMALL RESTAURANTS

I wish I could say that there is one neighborhood with the best mix of both chain and small, local non-chain restaurants. There isn't just one, but they come in sort of a cluster. I'm adding this because you may not want to drive around too much or too far after your beach day and before your chosen night time entertainment. If you begin with your GPS on whatever chain or diner for example that you want you can search from MidTown Miami to Miami Beach say around Lincoln Road to Byron Avenue. This is still below SOBE. It's calmer and cheaper with the most choice.

42. WYNWOOD EATING AND ART

I mentioned my Wynwood walls, one of my favorite things to see. You'll find more local tourists there in my opinion than those who come from other places. People scope them out during their lunch breaks and take advantage of the surrounding neighborhood restaurants.

You can find locals eating right there on a bench in front of a beautiful Miami mural.

43. THE MALLS

Mall food, yeah when you say that , it's not so appetizing, but our malls aren't your usual run of the mill mall with two anchor stores and a bunch of little shops of nothing.s. No, not Miami. Even our older malls that are still around have some great food courts.

Of course the ones in Miami can be found in safer neighborhoods from just South of Brickell avenue to Miami Downtown. You'll find anywhere from 15 to 30 restaurant shops in the court serving American food and all the tastes of Miami. Be ready for the portions and remember the rule of takeout that I mentioned before: split one between two to three people because you won't be able to put it in the car until you get back to your lodging. Some mall portions can weigh up to a pound or two.

44. SAFEST SOBE NEIGHBORHOODS BY WAY OF THE MOST DANGEROUS

Now, for the last few tips I want to tell you what the safest neighborhoods for you to travel through are in SOBE, MidTown and North Beach. This is important information you need to travel safely after dark here and have a late dinner before dancing, clubbing or simply driving back to your lodging.

South Beach in and of itself is not the safest area after dark. I'll be real with you. As of 2022 the city has ramped up the police presence and it has had some controversy attached to that. I want you to enjoy yourself and I won't sugar coat it. SOBE after dark is for really young people in their 20s looking for parties and adventure of every kind. I simply would not recommend it for families with kids or elderly.

The safest places to go in the evening for dinner if you decide you want the experience is According to Crime Grade dot org these are areas you just need to stay the hell away from day or night okay? Let's do it that way and just list the no-go areas.

45

Between 8th and 11th street

Any area at night just across from the Beach

Inland residential part west of the beach at any time, watch yourself

Just stay out of SOBE at night period at least by 8pm leave.

45. UNSAFE MIDTOWN AREAS

Midtown is quite safe and It boasts great affluent neighborhoods. However, remember that crime happens at night in the good neighborhoods too, so please keep all our belongings off the seats of the car and lock the doors. Don't get overconfident. Thieves look in these neighborhoods for obvious reasons.

Wynwood is mentioned by me as a favorite spot to eat lunch. At night there are tours through there and there are many art events. This is a great way to see art and locals and eat. However, there can be a fair bit of crime at night. So, plan this for the daytime unless there is an event on. Depending on what type of event it is, like something other than music, you will have more police presence and a more sophisticated clientele. So, less crime. Use your discernment.

46. UNSAFE NORTH MIAMI BEACH NEIGHBORHOODS

When we talk about malls and diners etc. North Miami Beach may come to mind and it may be suggested. Your concierge will certainly not suggest the area inland on the intracoastal over the bridge that attaches the beach at Sunny Isles beach to the mainland. That is around 169th street. There is a mall at 163rd street. You don't want to be there, and It's broken down and in a bad neighborhood day or night, and is not for tourists. Most of the locals don't bother.

Keep yourself from Haulover beach and south to Miami beach in the aforementioned safe areas. From over the bridge to the intracoastal there are restaurants on the water that we frequent in that safe area nearest to Eastern Shores. From there travel to past the mall and the Cloverleaf Freeway and start toward Miami Beach. Anything from Bal Harbor and Surfside then North Beach are the safest areas, but pricey.

47. EAT WHERE BRICKELL WORKERS EAT

The eateries that are in and around Brickell Avenue are made for and frequented by those that work in the prestigious offices and businesses surrounding it. If you deliver bad and expensive food, you get no business. Only in recent years has Brickell Avenue seen tourists in the number that they do now. The main people though are still those who live and work there.

I would suggest you explore this neighborhood for all it has to offer including the restaurants. The portions are normal and the pricing for lunch or dinner is a vast range. I would say between $13 per person to $30 per person and up for dinner depending on where you go. The experience is worth it to do just even just once to say you did. Just remember what I said about the portions and nouveau riche type restaurants you may get upset when you get a triangle of food and some garnish for that price range.

48. COCONUT GROVE

Coconut Grove or, The Grove as we call it is a small island of greenery and beauty that includes a blessed Indian ground there that sits in the middle of all the hustle and bustle in Miami and has a rich and sophisticated Latin culture mixed with other European cultures. The restaurants are spread out everywhere and this is a safe place to go and explore.

Sit among a canopy of beautiful trees and gardens. The lushness of it all will make you think you are definitely not in Miami, but in an oasis of nature and beauty. Eat, sit, observe and enjoy!

49. ARE RESERVATIONS NEEDED

If you want to eat like a native you may not be able to in the sense that we know the restaurants and the days and hours that may not be the most ideal. So, for you, yes a dinner reservation is necessary at formal sit down restaurants anywhere. Not all restaurants take them though because they are busy and won't hold a table. They make a better business by making it first come, first serve. So, ask the concierge or call and ask them early enough in the day once you've chosen a place.

50. TEN DOLLARS AND UNDER MIAMI

If you are here for a weekend or even a week and you aren't self catering you may be on a tight as hell budget. This is when you really taste Miami like the working class and that could expose you to the most culturally rich food in the place. The concept is simple, all the places that sell Cuban, Colombian or Caribbean food you can get away with $10 and below for big portions. However, understand that Cuban restaurants can be pricey too depending on where they are and what type. The others are less likely to have formal sit down restaurants, but I notice in the last decade that the Cuban restaurants have gone much more high-end in some areas.

Do the research and find a deal. Don't give up just because it's high-end. You can even find a local Groupon or something similar online or in those little coupon books. Be the culinary explorer you'll be surprised what you find here.

OTHER RESOURCES:

For those who are Map lovers and want a visual of the dangerous areas and the contrast between them and the safer areas. These are some maps from a few state websites so you can see patterns in the way we are structured. These are maps taken for Google.

I suggest that along with these maps that you Google "Dangerous Areas in____" and place the town or street where your chosen restaurant is. Google is rife with this information. The reason is a bit embarrassing to us as natives, but we accept that transience and tourism will bring crime. We would rather point out the areas you should not be than leave you with a fantasy image of Miami. If you want to see it like a native you have to understand the pitfalls.

The good news is, you aren't missing anything if you have to bypass a neighborhood with an advertised restaurant in it. You can find the same food elsewhere and enjoy it early or late without the stress so do the research and don't bother to chance it otherwise.

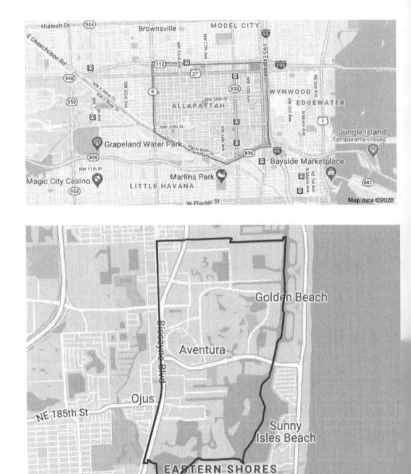

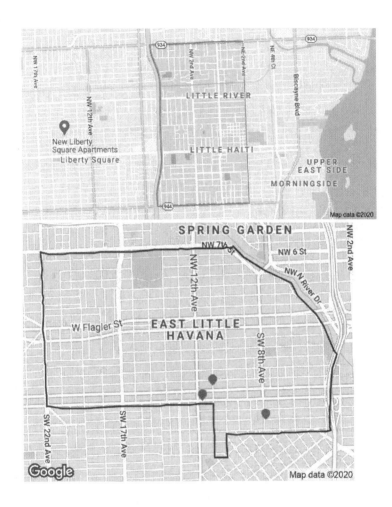

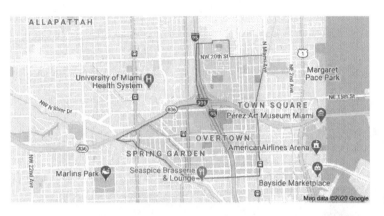

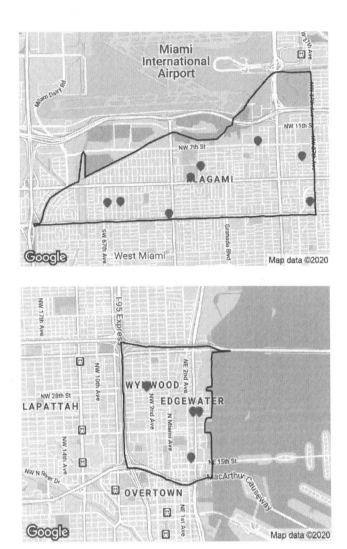

TASTE OF THE SEASONS

These are the markets that were mentioned. They have the best chance of being there still years from now. Miami has a transient atmosphere, but places tend to stay for decades or generations. We take that very seriously and try to maintain the culture of our magic city.

Government Center Outdoor Food Court
Location- Miami Proper

Time Out Market Miami
Location- Miami Beach

Smorgasburg Miami
Location- Wynwood, near the aforementioned Wynwood Walls

Mia Market Miami
Location-39th Street Miami Proper

Alton Food Hall

Miami Beach Proper

Legion Park Farmers Market
Biscayne Blvd Miami Beach Intracoastal Side

Bayside Marketplace
Miami Proper

Chamber of Commerce Miami
Miami Chamber.com/ Events

BONUS SECTION

Now that I've given you the facts about Miami eating, as a bonus I want to entice you as a native with a broader picture of what my eating outings are like. You see, we really eat with our eyes and when on vacation, we purchase the atmosphere and experience as well as the food.

I can honestly say that I include food in my life as a social event. Even when I am alone. I've been single for a long time and I've taken myself out on many occasions. Miami is a non-judgemental place in the way you eat and spend your time. Yes, there are snobby people. The Nouveau Riche { New Rich} are here and no shade, but there is a separate subculture. However, for the average person, especially the fabulous Hispanic and Caribbean communities here, there is a welcoming attitude.

THE SINGLE GAL'S EATING EXPERIENCE AS PER MY ROUTINE

First, no one here that represents the real Miami, the old-school immigrant-blessed town, is going to judge you for eating alone. In fact, here, and by using discernment as a tourist, it's a great opportunity to meet new people. I know folks that have met amazing people and shared food at a table with them very spontaneously. There are people that I am still in contact with from other countries and cultures.

WHAT AN EATING WEEKEND LOOKS FOR ME

So, the way my eating and entertainment weekend would look is as follows. This is the real deal from just me, one native Miamian. I am Italian American, born in NJ. So, I am not Hispanic and I am telling you this so you understand what perspective I'm coming from. Typically I'll decide at any given time where I want to be, for how long, and what I want to do while I'm there.

Bayside Marketplace is a favorite of mine. The address of this mega giant is 401 Biscayne Blvd, Miami, FL 33132 305-577-3344 This is a place that serves so many needs at once. Bayside is the shopping, dining and entertainment Mecca and so much more than just a mall. You can't really call it a mall because it takes some crazy acreage. You could spend the entire day there and still not experience everything.

Yes, if you like designer gear you can get it there, nothing in Miami survives as a shopping outlet that large and doesn't offer this. However, just like Miami itself I suggest not limiting the place or the town to one specific or several preconceived things.

65

There are shops and eateries for every taste and chains galore! If you want to experience Miami like I do or any native that is active in the city you'll want a varied experience. Places like the Bayside is a great way for you as a tourist to get a good taste of how we live and play. You can start in the daytime and have brunch at one of the many restaurants that offer Brunch food.

Then, shop till around 4pm and take advantage of everything from a Cuban Cafe to Bubba Gumps Shrimp Factory. For dessert and fun you can visit Sugar the sugar factory chain just to get the juices flowing for dessert. Bag up some of your favorite sweets to take home and venture off to a Gelato or Ice Cream shop.

You can find restaurants to suit any budget from $$ to $$$$$ It's an easy start for say $100 to begin with for one to two people as long as you aren't going to sit down or formal. You can sample all this for even less if you do what I do and choose a favorite for brunch or for dinner and the rest of the time, stick to the food court that's more like the malls. You can get quite a bit for $5-$7 and not break the bank.

You could go to the internet for research on their official Bayside website. You could also go to Restaurant Guru and read some reviews there. Walk around the food court and see who is there that you may like and take it from there. The point of eating like a native is living like us while you are here.

You should think like you're home, but in a different place. So that looks like this. What would you do if you were home with the way you budget your money and time? Transfer that to your Miami trip.

DO THE RESEARCH

Arrive at your destination
Take a walk around, see, smell and taste.
Deide what you want. A brunch or dinner.
Work out what your budget for the day will be.

The Oasis Wynwood is a food court that is a must do. As I stated before, it's safe in the day and at night. Just don't make it too late unless there is a calm and artsy event. The food court there has six main kiosks to choose from. Go to Oasis Wynwood website and go to the vendors tab to view the menus of all the kiosks there.

They are open Thursday to Sunday and closed on Holidays The events tab will tell you what's on for that month. It can get crowded and the lines can get crazy at the kiosks. I would not go the first time during an event when you are still new to Miami. There;s nothing that puts a bad taste in your mouth, (no pun intended) than a crowd and a line when you're starving. You've had a great day out and worked up an appetite. You're a stranger in a strange land and now you want to chow down on some great regional food. Always do your research about times and events so you don't get caught off guard.

Don't forget seasonal farmer's markets. They have great local fare from farms out west and local vendors that tempt your palate. Local honey, Cuban and Caribbean street food; and baked goods both sweet and savory are only the beginning. Eating like a native means you frequent these places for self-catering purposes as well as sampling the tastes of the town 100 percent.

Conclusion and Takeaways

You have a lot of information in this book from my perspective to think over. It may seem overwhelming, but I have taken the liberty to list the main takeaways to eating like a native below. They can be followed in order, the same way I instructed you to do when visiting Bayside for example. This way, you can refer to the end of the book here when you get started and you'll see just how simple and fun it can be so let's go!

Know your Taste and what you want to Experience. In other words, how much do you want to spend daily for food specifically? Are you apt to spend it on dinner or brunch, breakfast or lunch? You'll lose money if you aren't clear on this. Miami will gobble up a budget in a heartbeat if you aren't organized.

Understand the Food Type you want to Experience: The food type is essential to price especially. Do you want an immersive cultural experience and stick to street food and local Cuban and Caribbean restaurants? Do you want Nouveau Riche sort of food, what I referred to as the triangle of food with some garnish at a high price, or do you want to mix it up?

Adjust your Budget According to Choice: Now that you know your food type and your budget, review and adjust per person. If you do choose the Nouveau Riche type or the formal sit down restaurant on SOBE then you'll need at least $50 per person per night. Take into consideration the amount of time you'll be here too. I don't want for anyone to lose a lot of money early and end up missing out on the cultural food scene.

Do the Research Necessary: Go to the resources mentioned in this book, Chamber of Commerce of Miami for food events; the Groupons for Miami restaurants and where there are food truck events and remember the concierge. Use them!

Know the Safe Areas: Use the maps of the areas in this book to understand where the more dangerous areas are. Yes, some of them are fine in the day like Little

Havana and the main part of Little Haiti where the restaurants are but you can find the same food on the beaches and in the safe areas. Do not go to the places on those maps in the night, it's not necessary.

Create your Rout: This can be fun, but also quite necessary. Once you have your budget and the type of food you're looking for and the safe areas, find out the best way to get there. Gas is at a premium at the time this book is being written and it's not cheap here even when the economy is good so plan your route daily according to your preference.

Study your Coffee and Cuban Food Culture: Remember when you are ready for the cultural food scene that there are cultural customs discussed in this book. Study them and make it a great adventure to experience that. When you do, you'll be initiated as an honorary Miamian.

Congratulations on your new Miami journey. We love to have you who are interested enough in our culture to use a book to navigate it. Don't think for one minute that you are making it less spontaneous by doing so. You're not. Miami is a multicultural city unlike any other. For decades those from oppressed countries have sought asylum here and called this place home whether they wanted to or not and brought with them rich culture.

People from New York have come here for generations and will tell you that even though their city is also multicultural, it isn't the same as here in Miami. There was no established history of any one culture here. Miami was born from happenstance. You'll feel, see and taste it through the food, music, art and culture cultivated by that happenstance.

I hope your experience will be so rich that you come back time and again. Bring others with you and spread the word! We do want people here, not just anybody, I'm not gonna lie. People who appreciate the culture. Food is only a part of it, but Miami wouldn't be Miami without it. That's why I wanted to write this book about eating like a native.

Once you have the food down the whole culture comes to life for you.

You'll be sitting at a Cuban cafe and be charmed by the person beside you that drinks their coffee there every day. Or, you'll be at the Wynwood walls and eat the street food while you ponder the stories of the artists that created the street art on them.

One thing I want everyone reading this to do. Don't be too shy in reaching out to people sitting next to you at a public eating establishment or coffee bar.Use your discernment of course. You are a stranger in a strange land yet, understand that the Miami culinary culture is one of love. Eating and socializing go hand in hand especially with strangers. Go to the Domino Walk park and sit with the elderly gentlemen playing Dominos. Offer up a coffee and they'll let you sit and listen to their stories of how they landed in Miami. Some of them brought business to the area and are now retired. Their families run the places you just visited.

I promise, that if you use half of what's in this book you'll carry back home much to talk about and plan your next trip already!

READ OTHER BOOKS BY CZYK PUBLISHING

Eat Like a Local United States Cities & Towns

Eat Like a Local United States

Eat Like a Local- Oklahoma: Oklahoma Food Guide

Eat Like a Local- North Carolina: North Carolina Food Guide

Eat Like a Local- New York City: New York City Food Guide

Children's Book: Charlie the Cavalier Travels the World by Lisa Rusczyk

Eat Like a Local

Follow *Eat Like a Local on* Amazon.
Join our mailing list for new books

http://bit.ly/EatLikeaLocalbooks

CZYKPublishing.com

Made in the USA
Columbia, SC
04 February 2025